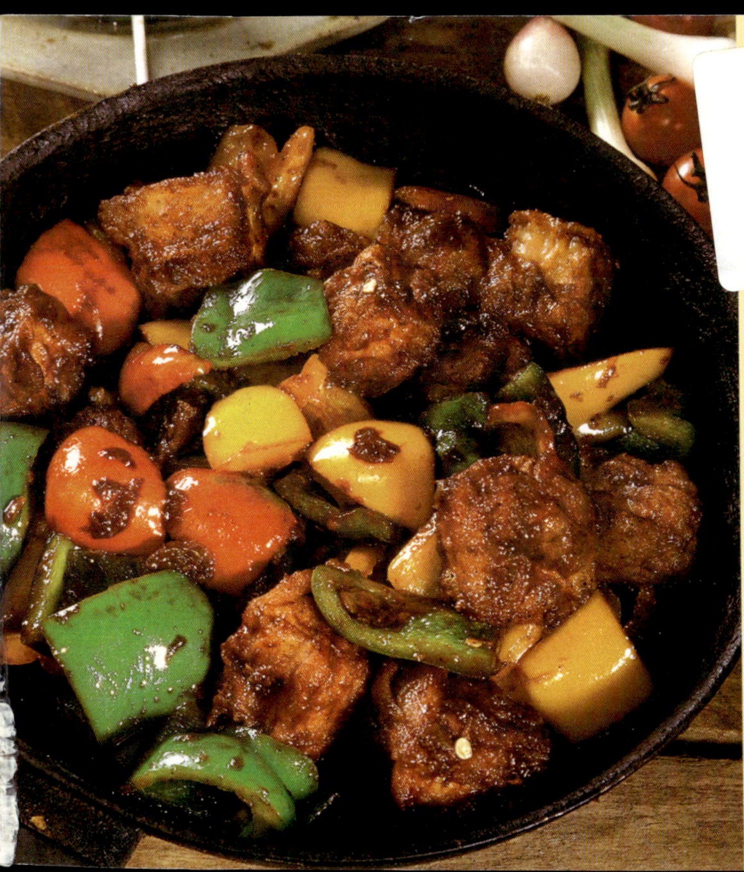

Chinese

VEGETARIAN
RECIPES

Nita Mehta

B.Sc. (Home Science)
M.Sc. (Food and Nutrition)
Gold Medalist

SNAB
Excellence in Books

Nita Mehta's
Chinese VEGETARIAN RECIPES

© Copyright 2008-2010 **SNAB** Excellence in Books Publishers Pvt Ltd

WORLD RIGHTS RESERVED. The contents—all recipes, photographs and drawings are original and copyrighted. No portion of this book shall be reproduced, stored in a retrieval system or transmitted by any means, electronic, mechanical, photocopying, recording or otherwise, without the written permission of the publishers.

While every precaution is taken in the preparation of this book, the publisher and the author assume no responsibility for errors or omissions. Neither is any liability assumed for damages resulting from the use of information contained herein.

TRADEMARKS ACKNOWLEDGED. Trademarks used, if any, are acknowledged as trademarks of their respective owners. These are used as reference only and no trademark infringement is intended upon.

Reprint 2010

ISBN 978-81-7869-209-8

Food Styling and Photography: **SNAB** Excellence in Books

Layout and Laser Typesetting :

N.I.T.A. ☎ 23252948 | National Information Technology Academy 3A/3, Asaf Ali Road New Delhi-110002

Published by :

SNAB Excellence in Books

Publishers Pvt. Ltd. 3A/3 Asaf Ali Road, New Delhi - 110002 Tel: 23252948, 23250091

Contributing Writers :
Anurag Mehta
Tanya Mehta
Subhash Mehta

Editors :
Sangeeta
Sunita

Distributed by :

NITA MEHTA BOOKS
3A/3, Asaf Ali Road, New Delhi - 02

Distribution Centre:
D16/1, Okhla Industrial Area, Phase-I, New Delhi-110020
Tel.: 26813199, 26813200
Bhogal: Tel.: 24372279

Printed by :

MEHTA OFFSET

Editorial and Marketing office:
E-159, Greater Kailash-II, N.Delhi-48
Fax: 91-11-29225218, 29229558
Tel: 91-11-29214011, 29218574
E-Mail: nitamehta@email.com
nitamehta@nitamehta.com
*Website:*http://www.nitamehta.com
Website: http://www.snabindia.com

Recipe Development & Testing:

Nita Mehta Classes/Foods
3A/3, Asaf Ali Road, New Delhi-110002
E-143, Amar Colony, Lajpat Nagar-IV
New Delhi-110024

Rs. 89/-

Introduction

A new cuisine called "Indian Chinese" has gained recognition; there are even restaurants which specialise in it, and the demand for recipes continues to grow.

I have written this book as a teacher, inspired by my students' demand for a simple-to-follow cookbook of Chinese food catering to Indian taste-buds.

I have explained the basics in detail – because without the basics, the final result can never be perfect! Learn about Chinese ingredients and how to use them; specialised equipment and techniques; the best way to cook noodles and rice; how to cut vegetables the Chinese way.

You will also find recipes for the best-known classics – those all-time favourites – with extra tips to help you avoid mistakes. So go ahead and treat your family and friends to a wonderful feast of twin flavours from two great cuisines!

Nita Mehta

C O N T

E N T S

Noodles & Rice   42

Vegetable Dishes   65

Chinese Ingredients and Sauces

SOYA SAUCE:
There are 2 kinds. One is dark and the other is light. Both are used for seasoning foods.

CHILLI SAUCE (RED OR GREEN):
This is a hot, spicy and tangy sauce made from red or green chillies, vinegar and seasonings.

VINEGAR:
It may be synthetic (acetic acid) or prepared from natural ingredients like rice, wine, sugar, fruits etc.

WORCESTERSHIRE SAUCE:
It is a thin dark, piquant sauce used to season dishes. It is made from tamarind, dry fruits, garlic, ginger and spices.

HOISIN SAUCE:
This is a thick brownish-red sauce. It is made form soybeans, spices, garlic and chilli peppers. It is used both in cooking and as a condiment.

OYSTER SAUCE:
Made from fresh oysters. Its special aroma and subtle sweetness enhance the flavours of most dishes. It is used not only in cooking but also as a condiment. Sprinkle a few drops over stir-fried iceberg lettuce & you will love it. It is best to refrigerate after opening.

BLACK BEAN SAUCE:
This sauce is made from fermented black beans. It has a pungent and salty flavour.

SESAME OIL:

Used as a flavouring, but not usually for cooking. It has a strong distinctive nutty taste & fragrant aroma. Only a small quantity is required. In cooked dishes a few drops of oil is usually added just prior to serving. It adds flavour to dips, salads and stir fry dishes.

STAR ANISE (CHAKRI PHOOL):

The dried, hard, brown, star shaped fruit has a fennel flavour. It is an important ingredient used in five spice powder. It can be substituted with fennel seeds (saunf).

DRY RED CHILLI:

Dry red chillies are easily available in markets. They are really hot. You can deseed them to decrease their heat.

FIVE SPICE POWDER:

An aromatic blend of 5 Oriental spices: 2 tsp peppercorns (saboot kali mirch), 3 star anise (phool chakri), 6 cloves (laung), 4" stick cinnamon (dalchini) and 3 tsp fennel (saunf). It is slightly sweet and pungent. Grind together to a powder, sieve & use.

CHINESE WINE:

There are many kinds of wine made from rice. Chinese wine can be substituted by ordinary dry sherry.

BEAN CURD/TOFU:

It is prepared from soya bean milk. It resembles Indian Paneer in taste & looks. Thus, you can substitute paneer with tofu.

SNOW PEAS/MANGETOUT:
They belong to the pea family and are used in cooking just like we use French beans. Whole pod is edible. Snap off the stem end of pea pod and pull the string.

SESAME SEEDS (TIL):
These tiny, teardrop-shaped, flat seeds are quite tasteless in their raw state but impart a wonderful nutty flavour after roasting. These are cream and black in colour. The taste and visual appeal of food is enhanced, when coated with these seeds.

AGAR-AGAR:
This is a dried seaweed. The white fibrous strands require soaking and are used like gelatine. It is used for puddings and as a setting agent.

SEASONING CUBE & VEG STOCK:
Use seasoning cubes mixed in water for making stock for soups and sauces. Seasoning cubes are available as small packets. These are very salty, so taste the dish after adding the cube before you put more salt. Always crush the seasoning cube to a powder before using it.

BEAN SPROUTS :
These are shoots of moong beans or soya beans. The texture is crisp. Add them at the end of cooking in a dish to retain the crisp texture.

BAMBOO SHOOTS:
Fresh tender shoots of Bamboo plant are available rarely, but tinned bamboo shoots are easily available in good shops.

AJINOMOTO (MONOSODIUM GLUTAMATE):
A white crystalline substance commonly known as MSG. It is used in Chinese cookery for enhancing the flavour of dishes.

CHINESE CABBAGE (WONGNGA BAK/NAPA CABBAGE):
It looks like a tightly packed cos lettuce. It has firm, pale green, crinkled leaves. If unavailable, ordinary cabbage can be used.

BOK CHOY (CHINESE CHARD):
A variety of Chinese cabbage. Also called spoon cabbage. It has dark green leaves with a white stalk and is used for stir frying. Both stalk and the leaves can be used. It is cooked only for a minute, so that it retains its colour and texture.

SHALLOTS
These are smaller onions, milder in flavour and belong to the onion family.

OYSTER MUSHROOMS:
These soft mushrooms are shaped like a fan. Delicious.

DRIED MUSHROOMS:
May be white or black. To prepare dried mushrooms for cooking, soak them in hot water for at least ½ hour to soften. They swell in size after soaking. Discard any hard stems. Cut into required size and use. They harbour a lot of dust and grit, so it is necessary to wash them well after soaking. They are added to dishes only for the last few minutes of cooking, to retain the crunchy texture. Used in soups and stir-fries.

About Noodles and Rice

Noodles are an important staple food in China. They are available in various varieties.

DRIED NOODLES:
They are made from plain flour (*maida*) or whole wheat flour (*atta*), with or without eggs. Straight as well as the coiled variety is available. They are usually cooked in boiling water with salt till almost done. Never fully done! Never overcook noodles as they turn thick and mushy on overcooking. They are cooked to an 'al-dente' stage (slightly *kaccha* with a little bite). Their cooking time is just 2 minutes for most of the varieties. Once they are strained, a little oil should be sprinkled on the boiled noodles to prevent them from sticking.

FRESH NOODLES:
Are available with vegetable vendors. They are sold loosely like a tangled ball of wool. Since they are fresh and moist, the cooking time is much shorter than the dried noodles. These are usually cooked in boiling water for about a minute or even less sometimes.

RICE NOODLES/RICE VERMICELLI:
Resemble long, translucent white hair. Rice noodles are just soaked in hot water for 5-6 minutes and then drained before use.

LONG/SHORT GRAIN RICE:
Polished white rice that forms the basis of most Asian meals. The usual method of serving rice is simply boiled but sometimes, for variety and richness, boiled rice is fried with other flavouring ingredients, such as sliced green onions/scallions, chopped white mushrooms and garlic.

WHITE GLUTINOUS/STICKY RICE:
This is a short-grain rice that sticks together when cooked because of high starch content. New rice can be used instead because the longer the rice is kept, the less sticky it gets. Glutinous rice is used in both savoury and sweet dishes. Is usually soaked in water for about an hour before cooking.

PARBOILED RICE (SELA RICE):
Parboiled rice (Sela rice) is preferred to basmati rice for Chinese cooking. This is a hard grained, yellowish rice which does not stick at all after cooking.

RICE FLOUR:
Ready-made rice flour is easily available in the market. Adding small amounts of rice powder to a batter or coating mix, makes the food crisp. In its absence, it may be substituted with cornflour in batters.

Chinese Cooking Utensils

WOK:

It is a deep pan, round bottomed with a single or double handle on the sides. A wok is ideal not only for stir-frying but deep-frying and simmering also. Chinese cook everything in a wok - from soups to rice to main course dishes. Choose a heavy bottomed one. Non stick woks are also available.

The wok comes in various sizes, <u>**the bigger the better.**</u> **The most functional size is the 11-12 inch (28-30 cm) round wok.** Sometimes it's fitted with a lid and an inner rack so you can steam vegetables and fish in it. The wok is deep, so you can boil rice and make soup in it. Its rounded sides provide enough red-hot surface for stir-frying foods quickly, usually in 3 to 5 minutes. The Indian kadhai is similar to a wok. You can use it in the absence of a wok. But I must tell you, buying a Chinese wok is definitely worth the investment!

WOK STRAINER:

A special strainer used to remove deep-fried pieces of food all together from oil at one time. Also useful for blanching food in hot water. Choose one which is slightly smaller than the wok. If not available, substitute with a single handle metal strainer.

STEAMING RACK (BAMBOO BASKETS):
An essential tool for steaming food, made of bamboo which allows steam to rise efficiently. Place the steamer basket on a wok with ½" of boiling water as a single steamer or stack in several tiers so various dishes can be steamed at a time.

Colander *(steel ki big channi)* can be used instead of the steaming rack.

LADLE:
Perfect for stir-frying and braising any food in a wok. The preferred ladle has a sturdy joint and an easy-to-hold handle.

CHOPPING BOARD:
The Chinese use a big heavy chopping board on which they chop almost everything with a broad flat knife. An ordinary wooden board of a moderate size can be used.

CHOPSTICKS:
These are thin long sticks, generally made of wood, and are used by the Chinese to eat with as well as to stir food while cooking.

13

Chinese Cooking Methods

STIR-FRYING:

Stir frying food, is to cook food on a high flame for a short period, **stirring continuously.** The ingredients are added to the wok in order of texture and cooking time. The hardest food is added at the start and the softer foods follow later, so stir frying of vegetables is done in sequence of their tenderness. E.g. onions are stir fried first, then french beans, then carrots, cabbage and so on. Each vegetable is stir  fried for a few seconds, before adding the next vegetable. Stir-frying requires good temperature control and is easily learned through practice. The heat should be progressively raised for the addition of other ingredients. Before you start stir-frying, remember to –

- Collect all ingredients required for the recipe.
- Slice all the veggies as required. Arrange in order of cooking.
- Marinade food if required, well in time.
- Measure liquids like oil, sauces and stocks.
- Blend any thickening agent (like cornflour) with stock or water and keep aside. Stir before adding to the wok.

PARBOILING:

To parboil means to partially cook food by boiling it briefly in water. Parboiling is used when vegetables differ in tenderness and texture. The tougher varieties are added to boiling water for a short time. They are then refreshed in iced water to set color and prevent overcooking. When the parboiled foods are cooked with more tender raw ingredients, the cooking time will then be the same.

DEEP FRYING:

Ingredients are cut into even-sized pieces and dipped into a batter such as flour & bread crumbs. These are immersed in hot oil to cover, until cooked.

- A slice of ginger can be added to indicate the oil's temperature for deep frying. If the ginger turns golden, the oil is right for deep frying.

- Marinated ingredients should be drained before dipping into batter for frying.

- Add small quantities of ingredients to the oil at one time. This maintains the oil's temperature.

- Add some fresh oil to used oil before reusing. This prevents oil from discolouring.

STEAMING BASKETS:

We require Chinese steaming baskets for steaming. These are made from bamboo and consist of two baskets and a lid. They come in various sizes. A new bamboo steamer should be soaked in water overnight before it is used the first time.

HOW TO STEAM?
Bamboo steamers are placed into a wok containing an inch or so of vigorously boiling water. Fill 1" level of water in a wok or a pot and bring it to a boil. Place the ingredients in the wooden steamer, stack them and cover tightly with a lid.

IF STEAMER BASKETS ARE UNAVAILABLE, THEN HOW DO WE STEAM?
Cook food by placing in a colander (metal strainer with big holes/ *steel ki badi channi*). Place the colander over boiling water in a slightly smaller pan. Cover the colander while steaming. Steaming helps retain flavour, shape, colour, texture and nutritional value.

Vegetable Cutting Methods

DIAGONAL SLICES : TO CUT VEGETABLE SLICES IN A SLANTING MANNER

The vegetables are cut into thin slices in a slanting manner in such a way that there are more exposed surfaces. Vegetables such as asparagus, carrots, celery or French beans are usually diagonally sliced.

SLICING : TO CUT COMPLETELY THROUGH THE VEGETABLE TO GET SLICES

The vegetables are cut into thin slices. The thickness depends on what is specified in each individual recipe. Tomatoes, carrots, mushrooms, onions etc. are sliced in quite a few recipes.

SHREDDING : TO CUT INTO THIN, LONG PIECES

The vegetables are cut into thin, strips or shreds. Spinach, lettuce, cabbage are all shredded. Carrot can be grated on the big holes of a grater to get shredded carrot.

DICING : TO CUT INTO VERY SMALL SQUARES

The vegetables are cut into dice or small cubes. The vegetables are first cut lengthwise into ¼ or ½ inch thick strips/fingers and several such strips/fingers are kept together and further cut into ¼ inch pieces.

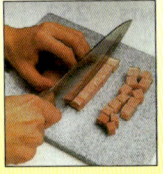

17

CARROT OR RADISH FLOWERS:

These flowers are usually seen in Chinese dishes. If the dish requires round slices of carrots, cut the carrot into round flowers instead. It enhances the look of stir fried dishes.

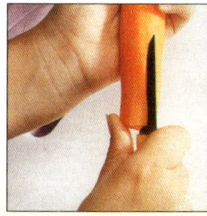

For carrot flowers, peel a thick, big carrot. Cut into two pieces to get 2 shorter lengths. Firmly holding the carrot upright, with a small sharp knife, make 1/8 inch broad and deep lengthwise cuts along the length of the carrot. Tilt the knife slightly to take out the thin long piece from the cut to get a groove. Make 2-3 more grooves leaving equal space between them. Carefully, cut the carrot into round slices as shown in the picture.

RINGS AND HALF RINGS: TO CUT THE VEGETABLES WIDTH-WISE INTO ROUNDS

Vegetables like onions or capsicums are cut width-wise to get rounds. The onion slices are then separated to give full rings. For half rings, cut the vegetables first into half and then cut width-wise to get half rings. When opened the half rings look like thin strips of onion and can be used as shredded onion also.

CARROT LEAVES:
Cut a carrot into very slanting slices. Cut a big carrot into very thin and very slanting slices. Make "V" notches on the side to get leaves.

TRIANGULAR PIECES:
cut a capsicum into 4 pieces lengthwise. Cut each piece at an angle, to get a small triangle of about 1". Cut the left over strip into half, giving a slant cut in the opposite direction at the centre to get 2 more triangles. Similarly you could get triangular pieces of tomatoes also. Coloured capsicums really look good when cut into this shape.

JULLIENE: TO CUT INTO THIN MATCH STICK-LIKE PIECES
The vegetables are cut into thin slices lengthwise. The slices are stacked together and cut lengthwise to get thin match sticks. Carrots and cucumber juliennes look good.

19

Simple Vegetable Garnishes

Always make vegetable carvings and garnishes before you begin a recipe.

VEGETABLE SHREDS:
They look beautiful on soups, salads and fried rice.
Cut the green portion of spring onion into very fine shreds. Shred as thinly as possible. Put the fine shreds into chilled water for a few minutes. Iced water will make the onion curl tightly.

ONION WATERLILIES:
They can be used to garnish stir-fries.

Use bulbous green onions or small white onions. Peel, wash & cut off green tops. Cut adjoining V-shapes around the onion, making sure the knife cuts through to the center. Separate the 2 halves by gently pulling apart; put into a bowl of iced water for several hours or overnight in the refrigerator to allow the onions to open out. Onions will keep for several days in water in the refrigerator.

CUCUMBER SPRINGS:

They can be used to garnish salads or any platter.

Use small tender cucumbers that have very few seeds. Cut the cucumber into approximately 3-inch pieces, discarding the ends. Poke a wooden chopstick right through the center of cucumber. Holding a small sharp knife at a slight angle, make the first cut all the way through to the center of the cucumber until the knife hits the chopstick. Continue cutting around the cucumber turning the chopstick as the cucumber is being cut until the end is reached. Remove the chopstick and pull the end of the cucumber gently so it forms a "spring". The ends may be joined to form a circle or the spring can be placed around a dish as a border. A slice of red radish placed between every second coil adds extra color.

Accompaniments, Sauces & Snacks

Hot & Sour Sauce

Makes ¾ cup

¾ cup water, 1 tbsp vinegar, 1 tsp pepper powder, salt to taste
1 tbsp cornflour, ½ tsp sugar, or to taste

1. Mix all the ingredients in a pan. Cook, stirring constantly till it boils. Simmer for 2 minutes on low heat. Remove from fire. Serve with any snack.

Schezwan Sauce

Makes ¼ cup

¼ of an onion - very finely chopped
1 tsp celery - very finely chopped

PASTE (GRIND TOGETHER)
3 dry red chillies - broken into small pieces
2- 3 flakes of garlic, 4 tbsp tomato ketchup, 1 tbsp oil
½ tsp soya sauce, ¼ tsp salt, 1½ tbsp vinegar

1. Mix the paste, onion, celery and ¼ cup water in a pan. Cook, stirring constantly till it boils. Simmer for 2 minutes. Serve at room temperature.

Green Chillies in Vinegar

Makes ¼ cup

¼ cup white vinegar, ½ tsp salt, ½ tsp sugar
2-3 drops soya sauce, 2-3 green chillies

1. Chop green chillies finely.

2. Mix all the other ingredients except green chillies. Heat on fire till it is just about to boil.

3. Add green chillies. Stir to mix well.

4. Remove from fire. Serve in a small bowl.

Sweet & Sour Sauce

Makes 1½ cups

½ cup tomato ketchup, ¼ cup vinegar
2 tbsp sugar, 1 cup water, 2 tbsp cornflour
½ tsp white pepper, ½ tsp salt, or to taste

1. Mix all the ingredients in a pan. Cook, stirring constantly till it boils. Simmer for 2 minutes on low heat. Remove from heat.

Sweet Chilli Dip

A thin dipping sauce which goes well with Chinese starters.

2½ tbsp sugar, ¼ cup water
1 tbsp honey, 1 tsp soya sauce
4 tbsp white vinegar, 1-2 tbsp oil
6-8 flakes garlic - crushed to a paste (1 tsp)
½ tsp red chilli powder
¼ tsp salt
1-2 fresh or dry red chillies - very finely chopped with a knife

1. Boil sugar and water till sugar dissolves. Stir continuously.

2. Add honey.

3. Add all other ingredients and remove from fire. Serve at room temperature.

Spring Rolls

With your first bite into these crisp and delicious starters the anticipation of the meal begins to build up.

Serves 4

SPRING ROLL WRAPPERS

1 cup plain flour (maida)

½ cup cornflour

½ tsp salt, 2 tbsp oil, a little water (chilled)

VEGETABLE FILLING

1 onion - chopped finely

8 french beans - shred diagonally

½ cup moong-bean sprouts, optional

½ carrot - grated

½ cup shredded cabbage

½ cup chopped capsicum

a pinch of ajinomoto (optional)

½ tsp white pepper

salt to taste, ½ tsp sugar, 1 tsp soya sauce

2 tbsp oil

1. To prepare the wrappers, sift plain flour, cornflour and salt. Add oil and water gradually, mixing to make a dough. Knead very well till smooth and elastic. Cover and keep dough aside for ½ hour. Make very small balls from the dough. Roll into thin rotis (rounds) 3"-4" in diameter. Heat a tawa & put 1 thinly rolled roti on it. Cook on both sides for 2-3 seconds. Keep rotis covered in a moist cloth.

2. For filling, heat oil. Add onion, cook till soft. Add beans, cook for a minute. Add carrot, cabbage, capsicum, ajinomoto, pepper, salt, sugar and sprouts. Stir for 1 minute. Add soya sauce. Check seasonings.

3. To assemble wrapper, spread a roti on a flat surface. Cut 1" from all the sides to get a square piece. Spread some filling thinly on the upper portion. Fold in ½" from the right and left sides. Holding on, fold the top part to cover the filling. Roll on to get a rectangular parcel; making sure that all the filling is enclosed.

4. Seal edges with cornflour paste, made by dissolving 1 tsp of cornflour in 1 tsp of water. Chill for ½ hour in the fridge, it gives better shape. Cover all with a plastic wrap/cling film to prevent drying out. Keep aside till serving time.

5. Heat some oil in a large frying pan for deep frying. Reduce heat and put the rolls, folded side down first in oil. Turn sides, to make it crisp and golden. Drain on paper napkins/ absorbent paper. Cut into 2 pieces with a sharp knife and serve hot with chilli sauce.

Momos

Delicately steamed mouthfuls of pure pleasure.

Serves 12

DOUGH
¾ cup plain flour (maida), ¼ cup cornflour, 1 tbsp oil, ½ tsp salt

FILLING
2 tbsp oil, 1 onion - finely chopped,

6 mushrooms - chopped very finely

1 tsp ginger-garlic paste, 2 green chillies - finely chopped

1 large carrot - very finely chopped or grated

2½ cups very finely chopped cabbage (1 small cabbage)

1 tsp salt & ½ tsp pepper powder, or to taste,1 tbsp vinegar

½ tsp soya sauce

You should Know...
The preferred way to steam momos or any vegetable is to steam it on medium high heat. Do not keep the heat low otherwise the water does not boil properly and enough steam is not formed, leaving them undercooked. For even cooking make sure that the momos are not touching the water when you place them in the steamer.

RED HOT CHUTNEY
2-3 dry whole, Kashmiri red chillies - deseeded and soaked in ¼ cup warm water for 10 minutes, 6-8 flakes garlic, 1 tsp saboot dhania (coriander seeds)

1 tsp jeera (cumin seeds), 1 tbsp oil

½ tsp salt, 1 tsp sugar, 3 tbsp vinegar, ½ tsp soya sauce, 1 tbsp tomato ketchup

1. Sift maida, cornflour and salt. Add oil and knead with enough water to make a stiff dough of rolling consistency, as that for puris. Keep in a cool place covered with a damp cloth for 30 minutes.

2. Heat 2 tbsp oil in the kadhai for the filling. Add the chopped onion. Fry till it turns soft. Add mushrooms and cook further for 2 minutes. Add green chillies, carrot & ginger-garlic paste. Mix well and add the cabbage. Stir fry on high flame for 3 minutes. Add salt, pepper, vinegar and soya to taste. Remove from fire and keep the filling aside to cool.

3. Take out the dough and form marble-sized small balls. Roll out flat, as thin as possible into small rounds of 2½" diameter.

4. Put 1 heaped tsp of filling on one side and fold over to form a semicircle. Stick the edges with water. Pleat the joint edges and then slightly fold the pointed ends to give it a little rounded shape. Keep aside.

5. To steam, place the momos in a steamer basket or a greased idli stand or in a greased colander (steel channi with big holes) and steam covered for 10 minutes. Remove momos to a plate.

6. For chutney, grind the soaked red chillies along with the water, garlic, dhania, jeera, oil, salt and sugar to a paste. Add soya sauce, vinegar and ketchup to taste.

Soups

Sweet Corn Soup

The addition of onions, carrots and cabbage gives this popular soup more depth of flavour.

Serves 6

1 tin (460 gm) cream style sweet corn, about 2½ cups
1 spring onion (hara pyaz) - finely chopped along with the greens
¼ cup carrot - finely chopped, ¼ cup cabbage - finely chopped
1 tbsp vinegar, 2 tbsp green chilli sauce, 1 tbsp red chill sauce
2 tsp level salt, ¼ tsp pepper, a pinch of ajinomoto
4 tbsp cornflour dissolved in ¾ cup water

1. Dissolve cream style corn in 9 cups water in a deep pan. Bring to a boil. Boil for 5-7 minutes.Add vinegar, green and red chilli sauce. Simmer for 1-2 minutes.

2. Add salt, pepper and ajinomoto to the soup. Add cornflour paste and cook for 2-3 minutes till the soup thickens. Add the vegetables- onions, carrot and cabbage to the simmering soup. Simmer for 1 minute. Serve hot.

Sweet Corn Soup with Fresh Corn

For fresh corn, grate 5 large corn cobs and pressure cook grated corn with 9 cups water and 1½ tbsp sugar to give 2 whistles. Keep on low heat for 6-7 minutes. Remove from heat and let it cool down. Proceed from step 2.

Hot & Sour Soup

Get ready for a taste explosion created by black pepper & red chillies balanced with vinegar and lots of vegetables.

Serves 4-5

CHILLI-GARLIC PASTE
3 dry red chillies - deseeded and soaked in water for 10 minutes
2 flakes garlic, 1 tsp vinegar, 1 tbsp oil

OTHER INGREDIENTS
2 tbsp oil, 1-2 tender french beans - sliced very finely (3-4 tbsp)
1-2 tbsp dried mushrooms or 2-3 fresh mushrooms - chopped
½ cup chopped cabbage
½ cup thickly grated carrot
6 cups water
2 vegetable seasoning cubes (maggi) - powdered, see page 8
1 tsp sugar, 1 tsp salt
½ tsp pepper powder, or to taste
1½ - 2 tbsp soya sauce
1½ tbsp vinegar
5-6 level tbsp cornflour mixed with ½ cup water

1. For the chilli-garlic paste, soak dry, red chillies in a little water for 10 minutes.

2. Drain the red chillies. Grind red chillies, garlic, vinegar and oil roughly in a small coffee or spice grinder.

3. If dried mushrooms are available, soak them in water for ½ hour to soften. Wash thoroughly to clean the dirt in them. Cut away any hard portion and then cut into smaller pieces.

4. Heat 2 tbsp oil. Add red chilli paste. Stir for a second. Add beans and mushrooms. Stir fry for 1-2 minutes on high flame. Add cabbage and carrots. Stir for a few seconds.

5. Add the water and the seasoning cubes. Add sugar, salt, pepper, soya sauce and vinegar. Boil for 2 minutes.

6. Add cornflour paste, stirring continuously. Cook for 2-3 minutes till the soup turns thick. Serve hot.

Talomein Soup

A light soup with carrots, cabbage and noodles.

Serves 4

4 cups vegetable stock or water mixed with a seasoning cube (see page 8)
½ carrot - peeled, 3-4 cabbage leaves - roughly torn
¼ cup dried noodles or ½ cup fresh noodles
½ tsp salt, or to taste, ½ tsp each of sugar, black pepper
1 tsp soya sauce, a pinch ajinomoto (optional)
2 tbsp cornflour dissolved in ½ cup water

1. Boil 5 cups of water in a large pan. Add 2 tsp salt and 1 tsp sugar to the water. Add peeled carrot to the boiling water. Boil. Keep on boiling for 1-2 minutes. Drain. Refresh in cold water. Cut into diagonal slices. Keep aside.

2. Mix stock, noodles, salt, pepper, sugar, soya sauce, ajinomoto in a pan. Give 1-2 boils.

3. Mix cornflour with ½ cup water in a bowl. Add this cornflour paste, stirring continuously to the pan boiling with stock.

4. Add carrots and cabbage. Bring to a boil. Remove from fire. Serve.

Wonton Soup

Serves 6

WONTON WRAPPERS

1 cup plain flour (maida), ½ tsp salt, 1 tbsp oil, a little water (chilled)

WONTON FILLING

½ of a small onion - finely chopped, ½ carrot - chopped very finely
8 french beans - chopped very finely or 1 cup chopped mushrooms
½ cup cabbage - finely chopped, a pinch of ajinomoto (optional)
½ tsp white pepper, salt to taste, ½ tsp sugar, 1 tsp soya sauce

WONTON SOUP

6 cups stock, (see page 41), 2 spring onions - chopped finely along with the greens
1 tbsp soya sauce, 1 tsp white pepper, 1 tsp sugar, ¼ tsp ajinomoto (optional)

1. To prepare the wonton wrappers, sift plain flour and salt.
2. Add oil and rub with finger tips till the flour resembles bread crumbs. Add chilled water gradually and make a stiff dough. Knead the dough well for about 4-5 minutes till smooth. Cover dough with a damp cloth. Keep aside for ½ hour.

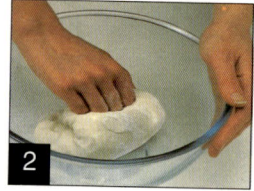

3. To prepare the filling, heat 1 tbsp oil. Stir-fry onions, for a few seconds. Add all other vegetables. Stir fry for 1-2 minutes. Add ajinomoto, pepper, salt, sugar and soya sauce. Mix. Remove from fire. Cool filling before making wontons.

4. Divide the dough into 4 balls. Roll out each ball into thin chappatis. Cut ½" from all the sides to get a square piece.

5. Cut into 2" small squares. (a) Place some filling in centre. (b) Fold in half by lifting one corner & joining to the opposite corner to make a triangle. Press sides together. (c) Fold a little again, pressing firmly at both sides of the filling, but leaving corners open.

6. Bring 2 corners together, and cross over in front of the filling. Brush lightly with water where they meet, to make them stick. Keep wontons aside. (The wontons may be folded into different shapes like money bags or envelopes).

7. To serve soup, boil vegetable stock, add the prepared wontons. Cover and cook for 12-15 minutes on low flame till they float on top. Add spring onions, soya sauce, pepper, sugar and ajinomoto. Simmer for 1-2 minutes. Remove from fire. Serve hot.

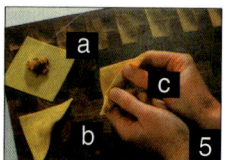

Vegetable Stock

A good stock should have a strong but properly balanced flavour – it is the foundation of good soup.

Serves 6 cups

1 onion - chopped

1 carrot - chopped

1 potato - chopped

4-5 french beans - chopped or ½ cup chopped cabbage

½ tsp crushed garlic - optional

½ tsp crushed ginger

½ tsp salt

7 cups water

1. Mix all ingredients and pressure cook for 10-15 minutes.

2. Do not mash the vegetables if a clear soup is to be prepared.

3. Strain and use as required.

4. Always serve soups, piping hot.

Note: Soup cubes may be boiled with water and used instead of the stock, if you are short of time.

Noodles & Rice

How To Boil Noodles

100 gm noodles, 6 cups water
1 tsp salt, 2 tsp oil

1. Boil 6 cups water with 1 tsp salt and 1 tsp oil. Add noodles in boiling water.

2. Cook uncovered for about 2-3 minutes only.

3. Remove from fire before they get **overcooked**. They should be crunchy with a little bite. Strain.

4. Leave them in the strainer for 2-3 minutes. Apply 1 tsp oil on the noodles.

5. Spread them on a tray greased with oil for at least 30 minutes.

43

Perfect Boiled Rice

Serves 2

1½ cups uncooked rice, 2 tsp salt, 6-8 cups water

1. To boil rice, clean and wash 1½ cups rice. Soak rice for 10 minutes.
2. Boil 6-8 cups of water with 2 tsp salt. Add rice.
3. Cook, uncovered, over a medium flame, stirring occasionally, until the rice is just tender but not **overcooked**. Drain the rice and let it stand in the strainer for 5 minutes. Fluff with a fork.
4. Spread on a tray and keep aside for at least 1 hour before you stir-fry it.

Haka Noodles

A basic dish of noodles and a variety of vegetables – mushrooms, bean sprouts and others – seasoned with garlic, red chillies, soya sauce and vinegar. Make it a great meal served with Manchurian balls in sauce.

Serves 4

CHILLI NOODLES

400 gms fresh noodles - boiled in salted water for just 2 minutes & spread in a tray, p 43

4 tbsp oil, 4-5 dry, whole red chillies - broken into bits

½ tsp chilli flakes or powder, 2 tsp salt, ½-1 tsp soya sauce

VEGETABLES

1 capsicum - shredded finely

1 carrot - cut into fine juliennes or match sticks

1 cup shredded cabbage

6-8 flakes garlic - crushed and chopped - optional

2 spring onions or 1 small onion - shredded

2 tbsp bean sprouts - optional

1-2 tbsp dried black mushrooms soaked & washed thouroughly or finely sliced
fresh mushrooms

1 tsp salt & ½ tsp pepper, ½ tsp ajinomoto - optional, 1 tbsp vinegar

1. Break red chillies into bits/pieces.

2. Heat 4-5 tbsp oil. Remove from fire, add broken red chillies and red chilli flakes or powder.

3. Return to fire and mix in the boiled noodles. Add salt and a little soya sauce. Do not add too much soya sauce. Fry for 2-3 minutes, till the noodles turn a pale brown. Keep the fried noodles aside.

4. To prepare the vegetables, shred all vegetables.

5. Heat 2 tbsp oil. Reduce heat and add garlic. Cook for ½ minute.

6. Add vegetables in sequence of their tenderness - onions, sprouts, mushrooms, carrot and cabbage stir fry for 2 minutes. Add vinegar. Add capsicum.

7. Add ajinomoto, salt and pepper. Cook for ½ minute. Slide in the noodles and mix well. Serve.

Chilli Garlic Noodles

You won't find veggies in these stir-fried noodles because they are meant to accompany a sauce-based main dish.

Serves 3-4

200 gm dried noodles or 400 gms fresh noodles, 3 tbsp oil, 1 tsp crushed garlic
3 dry, whole red chillies - broken into bits, ½ tsp red chilli flakes
a pinch of sugar ½ tsp salt or to taste, 2 tsp soya sauce, ½ tsp white pepper

1. Boil noodles and dry them as given on page 43.

2. Cut the dry red chillies into small bits or pieces.

3. Heat 3 tbsp oil. Add garlic. Stir.

4. Remove from fire, add broken red chillies and red chilli flakes.

5. Return to fire and mix in the boiled noodles. Add salt, pepper, sugar and a little soya sauce. Do not add too much soya sauce.

6. Mix well with the help of 2 forks. Fry for 2-3 minutes, till the noodles turn a pale brown. Serve hot.

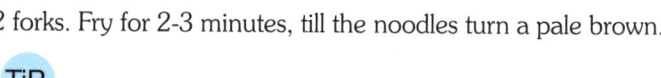

TiP

By drizzling soya sauce from the sides of the wok, a savoury aroma will be released and enhance the flavour.

Chow Mein

More than any other dish, chow mein has gained mass popularity. The noodles-and-vegetables mixture is coated in a well-seasoned, thickened sauce.

Serves 4

100 gms chow noodles

1 onion - shredded, 1 capsicum - shredded

1 cup shredded cabbage, 1 carrot - shredded

¼ tsp ajinomoto, 1 tsp white pepper

2 tsp soya sauce, ½ tsp cornflour

1 tbsp vinegar, 1½ tsp chilli sauce

2 tbsp oil, ¾ tsp salt

1. Boil noodles and dry them as given on page 43.

2. Heat oil. Add onions. Stir fry for ½ minute.

3. Stir fry carrots and capsicum for ½ minute. Add cabbage. Add salt, pepper, ajinomoto.

4. Add boiled noodles. Add vinegar and chilli sauce.

5. Mix cornflour with soya sauce. Add to the noodles. Stir fry for 1 minute. Add more soya sauce for a darker colour. Serve.

American Chopsuey

In this well-known speciality, the noodles are deep-fried to make them crisp. Shredded sweet & sour vegetables are piled on top and covered with more crisp noodles.

Serves 4

200 gms noodles
1 carrot - parboiled
8 french beans - parboiled
1 green chilli - shredded
1 capsicum - shredded
1 onion - shredded
¾ cup cabbage - shredded
½ cup bean sprouts
2 cups water, 5 tbsp oil
¼ tsp ajinomoto
½ tsp white pepper
4 tbsp tomato ketchup, salt to taste
1 tsp vinegar, 1 tsp soya sauce
3 tbsp cornflour dissolved in ½ cup water

1. Prepare crispy noodles as given on page 62.
2. Scrape carrot, string French beans.
3. Parboil them by dropping the whole carrot and french beans in 2 cups of boiling water with ½ tsp salt. Strain after one minute. Cool.
4. Shred all vegetables - capsicum, onion, cabbage, carrot and french beans.
5. Heat 5 tbsp of oil. Add sprouts and ajinomoto. Stir fry for 1 minute.
6. Add the remaining vegetables, green chilli, pepper and salt. Stir fry for 2 minutes.
7. Add soya sauce, vinegar and tomato sauce. Cook for ½ minute.
8. Add water. Bring to boil.
9. Add cornflour paste, stirring continuously. Cook till thick, for about 2 minutes. Keep aside.
10. To serve, spread crispy noodles on a serving plate.
11. Top with the prepared vegetables.
12. Sprinkle some left over crispy noodles on it.
13. Serve hot.

Chinese Chopsuey

Here is another variation of chopsuey, without tomto ketchup.

Serves 4

200 gms noodles
1 carrot - parboiled and cut into diagonal slices
8 french beans - parboiled
¾ cup shredded cabbage
1 capsicum - shredded
½ cup small florets of cauliflower
2 spring onions - quatered
½ cup bean sprouts
5 tbsp oil
¼ tsp ajinomoto
1 tsp white pepper
1 tsp sugar
2 cups water
1½ tbsp soya sauce
salt to taste
2½ tbsp cornflour mixed with 1/3 cup water

1. Prepare crispy noodles as given on page 62.
2. Scrape the carrot, string the french beans, remove the seeds from the capsicum and peel the onions.
3. Drop the whole carrot and french beans into 2 cups of boiling water to which ½ tsp salt has been added.
4. Boil for one minute, drain and cool.
5. Shred capsicum and quarter the onions.
6. Heat 5 tbsp oil. Stir fry the cauliflower, spring onions, bean sprouts and ajinomoto over a high flame for 2 minutes.
7. Add the remaining vegetables, pepper, sugar and salt.
8. Stir fry over a high flame for 2 minutes.
9. Add soya sauce. Cook for ½ minute. Add water.
10. Bring to boil and add cornflour mixed with ¼ cup water, stirring all the time, until thickened. Remove from fire.
11. To serve, put the crispy noodles in a serving platter and top with the vegetable mixture.
12. Alternatively, serve the crispy noodles and vegetables mixture side by side in a dish.

Vegetable Fried Rice

This mouth-watering family favourite is brimming with colourful diced vegetables.

Serves 4

1½ cups uncooked rice

2 tbsp oil, 2 green chillies - chopped finely

2 green onions - chopped, 2 flakes garlic crushed & chopped - optional

¼ cup very finely chopped french beans

1 carrot - finely diced, ½ big capsicum - diced

salt, pepper, ajinomoto - ½ tsp of each

1 tsp chilli sauce, 1 tbsp soya sauce (according to the colour desired)

1 tsp vinegar - optional

1. Boil rice as given on page 44 and spread out in a tray till absolutely cold.

2. Chop green onions, keeping the chopped green part separate.

3. Heat oil. Splutter green chillies. Stir fry garlic and onions, reserving the green part.

4. Add beans, then carrots. Stir fry for 1 minute. Add capsicum Add salt, pepper and ajinomoto.

5. Add rice. Add soya sauce and vinegar and chilli sauce. Stir fry for 2-3 minutes gently.

6. Add the green onions and salt to taste. Stir fry the rice for 2 minutes. Serve hot.

Fried Rice with Bean Sprouts & Nuts

Stir in extra crunch with bean sprouts, peanuts and almonds to make a delightful rice platter.

Serves 4

1½ cups uncooked rice
2½ cups bean sprouts
4 spring onions - chop white and green separately
¼ cup raw skinless peanuts (moong phali)
¼ cup almonds (badam) or walnuts (akhrot), 6 tbsp oil
¼ tsp ajinomoto, 2-3 tbsp soya sauce, salt to taste

1. Boil and drain rice as explained on page 44..

2. Heat 6 tbsp oil in a wok. Fry the almonds or walnuts and peanuts. Remove nuts from oil.

3. Sprinkle a pinch of salt on the hot nuts. Keep aside.

4. Heat the remaining oil in the iron wok and stir fry the white of onions, bean sprouts, ajinomoto and salt over a high flame for 2 to 3 minutes.

5. Add rice, soya sauce and spring onion greens. Stir fry over a high flame for 3 to 4 minutes.

6. Garnish the rice with the fried nuts and serve.

Crispy Noodles

The right way with the right tips gets the right results!

Serves 4

100 gm noodles
1 tbsp flour
2 cups oil for frying

1. Boil noodles as given on page 43.

2. Sprinkle flour on noodles to absorb any water present.

3. Heat about 2 cups of oil. Add half of the noodles.

4. Stir, turning sides till noodles are golden in colour and form a nest like appearance. Remove from oil.

5. Drain on absorbent paper. Fry the left over noodles in the same way. Cool and store in an air tight tin.

Chinese Steamed Rice

Steamed rice is made with just enough water to cook it so all the water is absorbed by the rice. On the other hand, boiled rice is cooked in plenty of excess water which is drained off once the rice is done.

Serves 4

1 cup uncooked long grained rice

2 cups water

1 tsp salt

1 tbsp refined oil

1. Clean and wash rice thoroughly. Soak for 10 minutes.

2. Heat water with salt and oil. When it boils, add the rice.

3. Slow down the fire, keep a griddle (tava) under the pan of rice and cook for about 15 minutes, until tender and dry.

4. Remove from fire and allow to cool. Separate the grains with a fork. Serve.

Vegetable Dishes

Vegetable Manchurian

Crisp, golden balls of vegetables float on a rich, hearty sauce.

Serves 6

MANCHURIAN BALLS

1 cup grated cauliflower

¼ cup diced carrots, ¼ cup finely chopped cabbage

1-2 slices bread - dipped in water and squeezed

1 tbsp cornflour, 1 tbsp flour (maida)

¼ tsp ajinomoto, salt and pepper to taste

2-3 tbsp milk, oil for frying

MANCHURIAN SAUCE

2 tbsp oil, 1" piece ginger - crushed to a paste

5-6 flakes garlic - crushed - optional

2 green chillies - chopped, ½ onion - very finely chopped

1 tbsp soya sauce, 1½ tbsp tomato ketchup

2 tsp vinegar, ½ tsp salt, ¼ tsp pepper

1½ - 2 tbsp cornflour

1 spring onion greens - chopped finely, to garnish

1. Chop carrot and cabbage very finely.

2. Mix all other ingredients of the balls, adding only 1 slice of bread first. (More bread may be added if balls fall apart on frying). Add enough milk so that the balls bind together easily. Make oval balls. Flatten each ball.

3. Deep fry 3-4 pieces at a time on medium flame. Reduce flame after the balls turn light brown and fry till cooked and brown. Keep the balls aside.

4. To prepare manchurian sauce, heat 2 tbsp oil. Add ginger and garlic. Fry on low flame for 1 minute.

5. Add green chillies and onions. Cook till they turn light brown.

6. Reduce heat and add soya sauce, tomato sauce, vinegar, salt and pepper. Cook for 2-3 minutes.

7. Add 1½ cups of water. Boil. Keep on slow fire for 2-3 minutes.

8. Dissolve cornflour in ½ cup water and add to the above sauce, stirring continuously. Cook till slightly thick. Keep the sauce aside.

9. To serve, boil the sauce. Add the balls to the manchurian sauce and keep on slow fire for one minute till the balls are heated through. Serve hot sprinkled with finely chopped spring onion greens with fried rice or noodles.

Sweet & Sour Vegetables

This easy recipe makes a winning dish every time!

Serves 4

1 carrot - cut into diagonal slices

4-5 medium florets cauliflowers

6-7 slices of cucumber

1 small capsicum - cut into ½" pieces

2 slices tinned pineapple

½ cup pineapple syrup or juice, 2 tbsp oil

1-2 green onions - cut into slices

½ tsp red chilli paste

1½ tsp roughly crushed or minced garlic

¼ cup tomato ketchup

5 tbsp vinegar, ½ tsp soya sauce

4 tsp sugar, ½ tsp salt or to taste

1 stock/soup cube - crushed

3 tbsp cornflour mixed in ¼ cup water

1. Boil 1½ cups water with ½ cup pineapple juice. Add carrot and cauliflower. Boil for 2 minutes.

2. Add tomato ketchup, vinegar, soya sauce, sugar, salt and stock-cube. Keep aside.

3. Heat 2 tbsp oil in a wok. Add white of onions, garlic and red chilli paste. Stir for a minute.

4. Add remaining vegetables - cucumber, pineapple and capsicum. Stir for a minute.

5. Add the vegetables in pineapple syrup to the wok. Bring to a boil.

6. Add cornflour paste, stirring all the time. Cook for 2 minutes on low heat. Serve hot with rice or noodles.

Veggies in Schezwan Sauce

The Schezwan region of China makes generous use of red chillies. Here different vegetables as well as tofu or paneer are tossed in a red hot sauce.

Serves 6

100 gms tofu or paneer - cut into ¼" thick triangular pieces

4-5 florets of broccoli or cauliflower, 4-6 babycorns - cut into 2 pieces lengthwise

1 carrot-sliced very diagonally and then cut into 2 pieces

6-8 leaves of bokchoy or spinach

1 capsicum - cut into 1" pieces

SCHEZWAN SAUCE

4 tbsp oil, 1 onion- cut into 8 pieces, 1 tsp red chilli sauce, 2 tsp soya sauce

2 laung (cloves) - crushed, 3 tbsp ready-made tomato puree, 2 tbsp tomato ketchup

¼ tsp pepper, ½ tsp salt or to taste, 1 tsp sugar, or to taste, ¼ tsp ajinomoto (optional)

1½ cups water mixed with 2 seasoning or stock cubes (maggie or knorr), see page 8

3 tbsp cornflour mixed with ½ cup water

PASTE

1 tbsp chopped garlic, 1 tsp vinegar

2 dry, red chillies - break into bits & remove seeds and soak in water for 10 minutes

1. If using bokchoy or spinach, trim the stem, remove any discoloured leaves. Tear into 2" pieces.

2. Boil 4-5 cups water with 1 tsp salt. Remove from fire. Add broccoli or cauliflower, baby corns, carrots and bokchoy or spinach. Leave veggies in hot water for 1-2 minutes and strain. Refresh in cold water and keep aside till serving time.

3. Grind all ingredients for the paste in a small grinder.

4. Heat 4 tbsp oil in a pan. Shallow fry the tofu till golden. Remove tofu from pan.

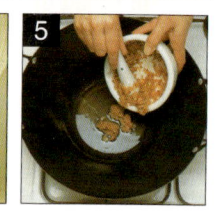

5. For the sauce, heat 2 tbsp oil again in the same pan. Remove from fire. Add garlic-red chilli paste. Stir till garlic starts to change colour.

6. Add onion. Saute for 1 minute. Shut off the flame add laung, tomato puree, ketchup, red chilli sauce, Soya sauce, pepper, salt, sugar and ajinomoto. Return to fire and cook for 1 minute on low heat. Add water mixed with seasoning cubes, give one boil.

7. Add cornflour paste, stirring all the time. Cook for 2 minutes on low heat. Remove from heat. Keep aside till serving time. To serve, heat the sauce. Add tofu, blanched vegetables and capsicum. Bring to a boil and simmer for 1 minute. Serve.

Chinese Sizzler

Arrange cutlets caged in golden noodles on one side, stir-fried veggies on the other. Pour a hot ginger sauce on top to create a sizzling sensation when it falls on the hot iron plate.

Serves 4

NOODLE CUTLETS

3 boiled potatoes - grated
1 carrot - cut into tiny cubes
1 capsicum - cut into tiny cubes
1 onion - chopped finely
1 tsp salt, 1 tsp soya sauce
½ tsp red chilli powder, 2 tbsp oil
6 tbsp bread crumbs
50 gms noodles - boiled

1. Heat oil. Stir fry onion for ½ minute. Add carrot and capsicum. Stir fry for 1 minute.

2. Add potatoes, soya sauce, salt and chilli powder. Mix well.

3. Remove from fire. Add bread crumbs. Mix well and shape into oval balls. Flatten them slightly. Dip in a thin batter prepared by mixing ¼ cup flour with ½ cup water.

4. Cover with boiled noodles. Deep fry till golden brown. Keep the noodle cutlets aside.

GINGER SAUCE

1 tbsp ginger paste, 2 tbsp oil, 2 dry red chillies, 1 tbsp vinegar, 1 tsp soya sauce
2 tbsp tomato ketchup
¼ tsp ajinomoto, ½ tsp salt, pepper
1 cup water, 1½ tbsp cornflour dissolved in ½ cup water

1. Grind red chillies with ginger to a paste.
2. Heat oil. Stir fry paste on low flame for 1 minute.
3. Add soya sauce, tomato ketchup, vinegar, ajinomoto, salt and pepper. Cook for 1 minute.
4. Add water. Boil. Add cornflour paste, stirring continuously. Cook till thick.

STIR FRIED VEGETABLES

¼ of a small cauliflower, parboiled - cut into florets
5-6 parboiled french beans - cut into 1" long pieces
1 carrot - parboiled, sliced or cut into leaves & flowers
1 onion - cut into fours & separated
salt, pepper to taste, ¼ tsp ajinomoto, a pinch of sugar, 2 tbsp oil
2 cabbage leaves - torn into big pieces - to serve

1. To prepare stir fried veggies, boil 3 cups water with 1 tsp salt and 1 tsp sugar. Add florets of cauliflower, beans and carrot. Boil for a minute. Strain and refresh in cold water. Keep aside on a kitchen towel.

2. Heat oil. Add onions. Stir fry for 1 minute. Saute for 2 minutes without stirring too much. Add all other vegetables, salt, pepper, ajinomoto & sugar. Saute for 2-3 minutes without stirring too much. Remove from fire.

TO SERVE

1. To serve the sizzler, brush the iron plate with some oil and heat it on the flame. Place cabbage leaves on the plate when it gets hot. Place the noodle cutlets on the leaf and stir fried vegetables on the side.

2. Pour the prepared hot sauce over it.

3. Fried potato fingers may accompany the sizzler.

Cantonese Vegetables

Chunky vegetables are spread out in a large pan for maximum exposure to heat in minimum oil. A light sauce is cooked in a few simple steps.

Serves 4

2 cups big chunks of cabbage

2 carrots - cut into round slices

2 onions - cut into fours

1 green bell pepper - cut into 6-8 large pieces

1 cucumber - cut into rounds (½ cup)

3 tbsp oil

1 tbsp light soya sauce, 2 tbsp vinegar

2 tbsp red chilli sauce

salt to taste, 2 tsp pepper

¼ tsp ajinomoto, optional

2 tsp sugar

4-6 tbsp cornflour dissolved in ¼ cup water

TO SERVE
rice or noodles

1. Wash and cut vegetables into big pieces.

2. Heat 3 tbsp oil in a big nonstick pan. Spread the vegetables in a single layer in the pan. Stir occasionally so that brown specks appear on the vegetables. Keep the vegetables crisp and crunchy. Take out the vegetables from the pan. Keep aside till serving time.

3. Put 3 cups water in the same pan. Bring to a boil.

4. Add all the sauces and seasonings.

5. Add about 4 tbsp of the cornflour paste first. Boil, stirring continuously. If the sauce is not thick enough, add more cornflour paste. Simmer sauce for 2-3 minutes. Remove from heat. Keep aside.

6. To serve, heat sauce. Mix the vegetables in the hot sauce and bring to a boil again. Serve hot with rice or noodles.

Spinach in Hot Garlic Sauce

This garlic sauce is hot, sweet and sour and brings out the best in greens. A dash of sesame oil gives the dish a distinctive finish.

Serves 2-3

150 gm spinach or bokchoy - cut into thick strips

GARLIC SAUCE
2 dry, red chillies - soak in water, drain and grind to a paste or ½ tsp red chilli paste
3 tbsp oil
2 tsp minced garlic
1 tsp soya sauce, preferably light soya sauce
1 tbsp red chilli sauce
2-3 tbsp tomato ketchup
1-2 tsp vinegar
½ tsp salt, ½ tsp pepper or to taste
¼ tsp sugar
2 tbsp cornflour dissolved in 1 cup water
1 tsp sesame oil - to finish

1. Wash spinach. Discard stems, cut the leaves roughly. If using bokchoy, use the leaf as well as the stem. Cut the leaf from the stem and use both.

2. Steam the spinach or bokchoy by keeping in a steamer basket or a colander over a pan of boiling water for 5 minutes. Keep the steamed greens aside.

3. Heat oil. Add garlic and red chilli paste. Fry for 1 minute on low heat.

4. Add the soya sauce, red chilli sauce and tomato ketchup. Stir.

5. Add the steamed greens and saute for 1-2 minutes.

6. Add cornstarch paste, stirring continuously. Add vinegar, salt, pepper and sugar to taste. Cook till a thick sauce is ready.

7. Finish with a tsp of sesame oil. Serve with steamed rice.

Note: Tofu and corn can be added to the greens for an interesting combination. A few toasted sesame seeds can be sprinkled at the time of serving. Also, you can add any vegetable of your choice to the sauce instead of the greens.

Cauliflower in Pepper Sauce

The triple use of pepper in this dish ensures an aroma and flavour that lives up to its name.

Serves 2-3

½ of a small cauliflower - cut into ¾" florets (1½ cups)
2 tbsp oil, a pinch of salt, ½ tsp pepper
pinch of ajinomoto (optional)
greens of 1 spring onion - cut into ½" pieces

SAUCE
1 white portion of spring onion - chopped
¼ tsp ginger paste, ¼ tsp chopped garlic
6 peppercorns (saboot kali mirch)
1 tsp freshly ground black pepper
½-1 tsp soya sauce, 1 tsp vinegar
¼- ½ tsp salt or to taste
a pinch of ajinomoto, 2 tbsp oil

MIX TOGETHER
1½ cups water, 1 vegetable seasoning cube (maggi or knorr)

PASTE

1¾ tbsp cornflour, ¼ cup water

1. Cut cauliflower into ¾" florets with a little stalk.

2. Chop white portion of spring onion. Cut the green portion into ½" pieces.

3. Crush 1 vegetable seasoning cube and add to 1½ cups of water in a saucepan. Give one boil and keep aside.

4. Mix cornflour with water to a smooth paste. Keep aside.

5. Heat 2 tbsp oil in a wok or a kadhai and add cauliflower.

6. Stir fry the cauliflower for 3-4 minutes on medium heat till brown specks appear on the cauliflower.

7. Add a pinch of salt, ¼ tsp pepper and pinch of ajinomoto. Keep aside.

8. Heat 2 tbsp oil. Reduce heat and add white portion of spring onion, ginger paste, chopped garlic and peppercorns. Cook till garlic changes colour. Reduce heat, add black pepper, soya sauce, vinegar, salt and ajinomoto.

9. Add water mixed with a seasoning cube. Give one boil.

10. Add the prepared cornflour paste. Cook till sauce thickens slightly. Keep aside till serving time. Add fried cauliflower and greens of spring onion. Remove from fire. Serve hot.

Potato Strings in Ginger Sauce

Everyone loves deep-fried potato strings. Here they are combined with capsicum strips and tossed in a tingling ginger sauce just before serving.

Serves 4

2 potatoes - sliced very thinly to get juliennes
3 capsicums - sliced very thinly to get juliennes
3½ tsp ginger paste
2 onions - chopped finely
1 tsp salt, ¾ tsp pepper
1 tsp soya sauce
2 tsp tomato ketchup
2¼ tbsp cornflour mixed with ½ cup water
2 vegetable seasoning cubes (maggi, knorr or any other)

1. To make stock with cubes, crush 2 vegetable seasoning cubes and mix with 2 cups of water in a saucepan. Give one boil and keep aside.

2. Peel potatoes. Wash and cut each into thin slices, and cut each slice further into very thin fingers to get juliennes. Wipe dry on a kitchen towel. Put in a bowl and sprinkle 2-3 tbsp cornflour to absorb the excess moisture. Mix well. Cut capsicum also to get thin fingers.

3. Heat oil in a wok. Deep fry some shredded potatoes at a time. Fry in batches till golden brown and crisp. Drain on paper napkins. Keep them spread out. Repeat to fry the remaining potato strings.

4. Heat 4 tbsp oil in a kadhai. Add ginger paste. Cook on low flame for 1-2 minutes.

5. Add the chopped onion, cook till golden. Add salt and pepper. Stir fry for a few seconds. Add soya sauce, ketchup. Add the prepared seasoning water or stock. Give one boil.

6. Add cornflour paste, stir till the sauce just starts to get thick. Remove from fire and keep aside till serving time. At serving time, bring the sauce to a boil. Simmer for 1-2 minutes. Add fried potatoes and capsicum. Mix well and serve hot immediately.

Cauliflower Manchurian

These deep-fried balls are shaped out of grated cauliflower and crusted with breadcrumbs. A sharp, smooth sauce creates the right combination.

Serves 4

MANCHURIAN BALLS

2 tsp cornflour, 2 tsp flour

1½ cups grated cauliflower

1 tsp dry red chilli paste

½ tsp baking powder

salt to taste

¼ cup milk

2 tbsp bread crumbs

MANCHURIAN SAUCE

1½ tbsp oil, 1 tsp garlic paste

2 green chillies, 2 tsp soya sauce

2 tsp vinegar, 1½ tbsp tomato ketchup

½ tsp salt, 1½ cups water, 2 tbsp cornflour dissolved in ½ cup water

green of 2 spring onions - chopped

1. Mix flour, cornflour, baking powder, red chilli paste and salt to taste. Make a thick batter with milk.

2. Add cauliflower and mix well. Shape into flat balls.

3. Roll in bread crumbs and deep fry. Keep aside.

4. To prepare the sauce, heat 2 tbsp oil. Stir fry garlic and green chillies for ½ minute on low flame.

5. Add soya sauce, tomato sauce and vinegar. Cook for ½ minute. Add water. Boil.

6. Add cornflour paste, stirring continuously. Cook till the sauce thickens. Add spring onion tops.

7. To serve, boil the sauce. Add balls, keep on low flame for ½ minute. Serve hot.

Chilli Paneer

Golden, batter-fried cubes of paneer are stir-fried with hot green chillies – so quick, easy and tasty!

Serves 4

1½ tbsp cornflour, 1½ tbsp flour (maida)
½ tsp salt, 125 gms paneer
2 tsp soya sauce, 1 tbsp chilli sauce
2½ tbsp tomato sauce, ½ tbsp vinegar
4-5 green chillies - slit lengthwise
4-5 flakes crushed garlic - optional, 1 tbsp chopped coriander
¼ tsp each of ajinomoto, sugar, ¼ tsp each of salt, pepper

1. Mix flour, cornflour and salt. Add enough water, about 3 tbsp, to make a batter of a thick pouring consistency, such that it coats the paneer.

2. Cut paneer into ¾" cubes. Dip each piece in the batter and deep fry till golden brown.

3. Heat 2 tbsp oil. Fry the green chillies and garlic. Reduce heat. Add salt, pepper, sugar and ajinomoto. Add soya sauce, chilli sauce, tomato sauce and vinegar. Stir.

4. Add the fried paneer and coriander. Mix well.

5. Serve hot. A tooth pick may be inserted in each piece to serve it as a snack.

Cottage Cheese in Hot Garlic Sauce

This main dish has plenty of sauce to soak into rice, and large servings of protein-rich cottage cheese. It has a never-fail appeal that your guests will go for.

Serves 4

125 gm cottage cheese (paneer)

2 tbsp cornflour, 2 tbsp flour (maida)

¼ tsp pepper, ajinomoto & salt

4 tbsp water, 1 cup garlic sauce, as given on page 82

2 tbsp chopped spring onion greens - to garnish

1. Cut cottage cheese in big rectangular cubes.

2. Make a thick batter by mixing cornflour, flour, salt, pepper and ajinomoto with water.

3. Dip paneer pieces and deep fry to a golden colour.

4. Prepare garlic sauce as given on page 82.

5. At serving time, heat sauce. Add paneer and bring to a boil.

6. Transfer to a serving dish and garnish with greens of spring onion.

Stir Fried Vegetables

Parboiled vegetables can stand at the start-start line with others – they all reach the finish together to win a gold medal for freshness and flavour.

¼ of a small cauliflower or broccoli - cut into florets
5-6 parboiled french beans - cut into 1" long pieces
3 whole flakes of garlic - sliced thinly
1 onion - cut into fours & separated
1 carrot - cut into fingers
2 cabbage leaves - torn into big pieces
¼ tsp salt, ¼ tsp pepper to taste, 1 tbsp oil
2-3 tbsp ready-made stir fry sauce

1. Boil 4 cups water with 1 tsp salt. Add beans, cauliflower and carrots. Boil for 2 minutes till slightly soft. Remove from fire and strain. Pat dry and keep aside.

2. Heat oil. Add garlic and onions. Stir fry for 2-3 minutes.

3. Add cauliflower or broccoli. Stir fry for 2 minutes.

4. Add all other vegetables and ingredients. Remove from fire.

Glossary of Names/Terms

HINDI OR ENGLISH NAMES USED IN INDIA	ENGLISH NAMES AS USED IN USA/UK/ OTHER COUNTRIES
Chilli powder	Red chilli powder, Cayenne pepper
Cornflour	Cornstarch
Coriander, fresh	Cilantro
Dalchini	Cinnamon
French beans	Green beans
Gajar	Carrots
Gobhi	Cauliflower
Hara Dhania	Cilantro/fresh or green coriander
Hari Gobhi	Broccoli
Hari Mirch	Green hot peppers, green chillies, serrano peppers
Illaichi	Cardamom
Imli	Tamarind
Jeera Powder	Cumin seeds
Kadhai/Karahi	Wok
Kaju	Cashewnuts

INTERNATIONAL CONVERSION GUIDE

These are not exact equivalents; they've been rounded-off to make measuring easier.

WEIGHTS & MEASURES

METRIC	IMPERIAL
15 g	½ oz
30 g	1 oz
60 g	2 oz
90 g	3 oz
125 g	4 oz (¼ lb)
155 g	5 oz
185 g	6 oz
220 g	7 oz
250 g	8 oz (½ lb)
280 g	9 oz
315 g	10 oz
345 g	11 oz
375 g	12 oz (¾ lb)
500 g	16 oz (1 lb)
1 kg	30 oz (2 lb)

LIQUID MEASURES

METRIC	IMPERIAL
30 ml	1 fluid oz
60 ml	2 fluid oz
100 ml	3 fluid oz
125 ml	4 fluid oz
150 ml	5 fluid oz (¼ pint/1 gill)
190 ml	6 fluid oz
250 ml	8 fluid oz
300 ml	10 fluid oz (½ pint)
500 ml	16 fluid oz
600 ml	20 fluid oz (1 pint)
1000 ml	1¾ pints

CUPS & SPOON MEASURES

METRIC	IMPERIAL
1 ml	¼ tsp
2 ml	½ tsp
5 ml	1 tsp
15 ml	1 tbsp

HELPFUL MEASURES

METRIC	IMPERIAL
3 mm	1/8 in
6 mm	¼ in
1 cm	½ in
2 cm	¾ in
2.5 cm	1 in
5 cm	2 in
6 cm	2½ in
8 cm	3 in
10 cm	4 in
13 cm	5 in
15 cm	6 in
25 cm	10 in
28 cm	11 in
30 cm	12 in (1ft)

NITA MEHTA
COOKERY CLUB

Become a MEMBER

Get FREE Cookbooks

www.nitamehta.com

CLICK HERE

Become a Member
Get Free Cookbooks

nita mehta.com
Recipes, Cook Books, Classes & Much more.

Book Search

About Nita Mehta
International Award Winner
Reviews & Comments
Order outside India

Cooking Tips
Self Help & Fitness
Recipe of the Week
Business Opportunities
Interactive Events

Cookery Books
Indian Cuisine
International Cuisine
Low Calorie Books
Microwave Cooking
Other Books
Hindi Books
Complete List of Books

Welcome !

Where to Buy | Ask Nita Mehta

What's New

Nita Mehta's
Cooking for
Growing
Children

Cookery Classes

Meet
the author
& enjoy
interactive
cookery
sessions

NITA MEHTA

Cook Books by Nita Mehta

Children Books

Members Area

Login
Password

login

Register   Forgot Password

Register at : www.nitamehta.com

Now you can buy Nita Mehta & Tanya Mehta books with your credit card

Buy Online at www.nitamehta.com